The Dirty Thirties

Sean Price

Chicago, Illinois

Customer Service 888-363-4266

Visit our website at www.heinemannraintree.com

Designed by Michelle Lisseter, Kim Miracle, and Bigtop
Printed in China

16 15 14
10 9 8 7 6 5 4 3

**Library of Congress
Cataloging-in-Publication Data**

Price, Sean.
   The dirty thirties : documenting the Dust Bowl / Sean Price.
      v. cm. -- (American history through primary sources)
   Includes bibliographical references and index.
   Contents: Nature's fury -- Heading to California -- Telling the Okies'
story -- Getting a new deal -- Quilts of the Dust Bowl.
   ISBN 1-4109-2416-5 (hc) -- ISBN 1-4109-2427-0 (pb)
   1. Dust Bowl Era, 1931-1939--Juvenile literature. 2. Great Plains--Social
conditions--Juvenile literature. 3. Dust storms--Great Plains--History--20th century--Juvenile literature. 4. Depressions--1929--Great Plains--Juvenile literature.
5. Migration,
Internal--United States--History--20th century--Juvenile literature. 6.
West (U.S.)--History--1890-1945--Juvenile literature.
I. Title. II. Series.
   F595.P94 2007
   978'.03--dc22
                                        2006010686

13 digit ISBNs
978-1-4109-2416-2 (hardcover)
978-1-4109-2427-8 (paperback)

Acknowledgments
The author and publisher are grateful to the following for permission to reproduce copyright material: Bettmann/Corbis **p. 9**; Corbis **pp. 5**, **17** (John Springer Collection), **20–21**; Getty Images **pp. 6**, **11**; Library of Congress Prints and Photographs Division **pp. 7**, **12**, **15**, **18**, **19**, **23**, **24**, **25**, **26**, **27**; Time Life Pictures/Getty Images **pp. 28**, **29**.

Cover photograph of a young cotton picker in Kern County migrant camp, California, photographed by Dorothea Lange reproduced with permission of the Library of Congress Prints and Photographs Division.

Photo research by Tracy Cummins
Illustrations by Darren Lingard

The publishers would like to thank Nancy Harris and Joy Rogers for their assistance in the preparation of this book.

Every effort has been made to contact copyright holders of any material reproduced in this book. Any omissions will be rectified in subsequent printings if notice is given to the publishers.

Contents

Some words are printed in bold, **like this**. You can find out what they mean on page 30. You can also look in the box at the bottom of the page where they first appear.

Nature's Fury

In the 1930s, dust storms swept across the United States. Giant black clouds appeared. The storms blew from Texas to South Dakota. They dumped huge amounts of dust on towns and farms. The dust hid the Sun. Street lamps were used during the day. So were car headlights. People and animals could choke to death in clouds of dust.

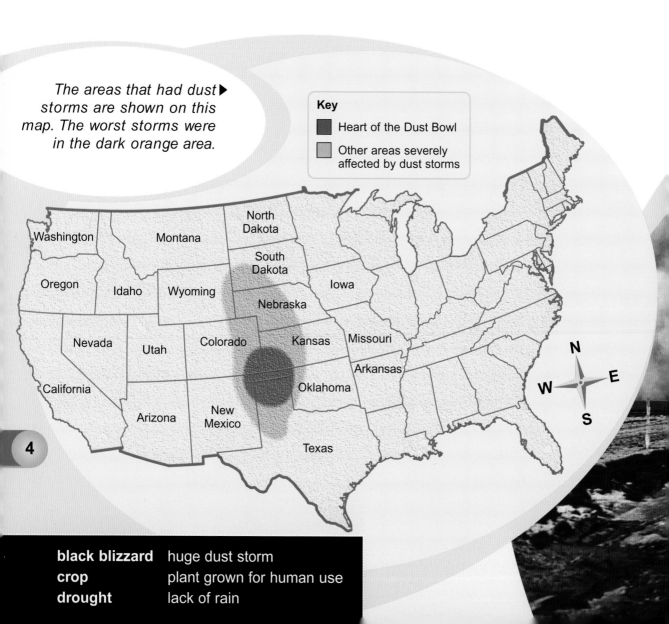

The areas that had dust storms are shown on this map. The worst storms were in the dark orange area. ▶

Key

■ Heart of the Dust Bowl

■ Other areas severely affected by dust storms

Washington
Montana
North Dakota
South Dakota
Oregon
Idaho
Wyoming
Iowa
Nebraska
Nevada
Utah
Colorado
Kansas
Missouri
Arkansas
California
Oklahoma
Arizona
New Mexico
Texas

N
W — E
S

black blizzard	huge dust storm
crop	plant grown for human use
drought	lack of rain

People called these storms **black blizzards**. A blizzard is a heavy, windy snowstorm. "Black blizzards" were storms of dust and dirt. The Midwest suffered from a **drought**. A drought is lack of rain. The winds blew. The farm **crops** died. People could not keep soil from blowing away.

People called this time the Dust Bowl. It lasted from 1930 to 1941. The Dust Bowl changed the lives of millions of Americans.

▼ Dust storms like this were called black blizzards.

Life in the Dust Bowl

The Dust Bowl started in 1930. The **black blizzards** became bigger and bigger each year. The worst black blizzard happened on April 14, 1935. Dust got into everything. People put wet sheets over windows. But dust still got into their houses.

Some black blizzards buried cars and houses. The *Saturday Evening Post* magazine described one farm after a storm:

> In the farmyard, fences, machinery, and trees were gone, buried. The roofs of sheds stuck out through drifts [of dust] deeper than a man is tall.

This photo shows ▼ a house buried under dust. This was caused by a black blizzard.

Great Depression   period when many Americans could not find jobs. It lasted from 1929 to 1941.

▼*This young boy tries to keep the dust out of his eyes.*

The Dust Bowl was hardest on farmers (see the map on page 4). It was a time when jobs were very hard to find. These farmers had already been out of work. This time was called the **Great Depression**. The Depression started in 1929.

Heading to California

The Dust Bowl made it tough to grow **crops** (plants). In 1931 another **disaster** struck. It was a terrible event. Billions of grasshoppers suddenly appeared in the Midwest. The grasshoppers ate the few crops that were left. Soon, "For Sale" signs appeared on many farms.

Flora Robertson▶ wrote a poem about going to California.

"Why We Come to Californy" by Flora Robertson

Here comes the dust-storm
Watch the sky turn blue.
You better git out quick
Or it will smother you.

Here comes the grasshopper,
He comes a-jumpin' high.
He jumps away across the state
An' never bats an eye…

Californy, Californy,
Here I come too.
With a coffee pot and skillet,
I'm a-comin' to you!

8

disaster   terrible event
Okie   person fleeing the Dust Bowl

Many people moved to California. They had heard that California had farm jobs. People came from Arkansas and Missouri. They came from Texas. They came from a lot of states. Since so many came from Oklahoma, people called them all **Okies**.

▼ *Many people left home for California during the Dust Bowl.*

Jalopies on the road

Most **Okies** had been farmers. They had worked hard all their lives. Now, dust storms and **drought** (lack of rain) had taken away their land. They were poor and needed help. Mostly, they needed jobs.

The Okies headed to California in search of jobs. Okies piled everything they had into their **jalopies**. Jalopies were old, beat-up cars. Many of these overloaded cars could barely run.

Tires blew out. Engine parts broke. The journey was at least 1,000 miles (1,600 kilometers). That took a lot of gas. Most Okie families kept their slow-moving cars running. Still, broken-down jalopies were a common sight.

The great escape

At least one million people left their farms during the Dust Bowl years. Many of these people went to California. The nice weather there made it a good place to grow **crops**.

jalopy   old, beat-up car

▲ Many Okies traveled in old cars that broke down a lot.

It took a long time to ▲
get to California. This
family rests on the
side of the road.

Life in an Okieville

The **Okies'** journey to California usually took three or four days. Few had money for hotels or restaurants. Instead, they camped beside the road. They cooked in the camps. Many beat-up **jalopies** broke down on the way. They often broke down in California's Mojave Desert. It was scorching hot there during the day.

Getting to California was hard. Finding work there was hard too. The first groups of Okies found jobs fairly easily. There were plenty of **crops** (plants) to pick in California. Others had a difficult time. They became **migrant** farmworkers. A migrant is someone who moves from place to place a lot.

It was hard to find cheap places to stay. Okies often ended up in small camps made of tents or **shacks**. A shack is a small, poorly built cabin. These camps were called **Okievilles**. There was never enough food. Illness was common. "We lived like animals," one Okie remembered.

migrant   someone who moves a lot from place to place
Okieville   small camp where Okies lived. They were made up of tents and shacks.
shack   poorly built cabin

In the fields

Picking **crops** was hard work. People bent down for twelve to fourteen hours a day to pick peas. Cotton plants had sharp edges. They made fingers bleed. For that, workers got paid between one dollar and five dollars a day. Usually it was closer to one dollar.

Whole families joined in. Children worked before or after school. Often they skipped school completely. Dale Gene Scales began working in third grade. He remembered:

"As soon as I got home after school let out, I would go out in the fields and pick cotton. My mom would make me a peanut butter and jelly sandwich. I would swing my [cloth] sack over my back, and I would go out into the fields until it got dark."

Money Fact

In the 1930s, one dollar bought more than it does today. A basketball cost one dollar. A new bike cost eleven dollars.

▼Even young people had to work hard.

15

Telling the Okies' Story

Woody Guthrie was born in Okemah, Oklahoma. He worked as a singer when the Dust Bowl began. In 1937 Guthrie left for California. He saw how much the **Okies** had suffered. Guthrie wrote songs about what he saw. Some songs poked fun at people who treated Okies badly. The "do re mi" in this song means "money":

"Do Re Mi"

Oh, if you ain't got the do re mi, folks,
you ain't got the do re mi,
Why, you better go back to beautiful Texas,
Oklahoma, Kansas, Georgia, Tennessee.
California is a garden of Eden,
a paradise to live in or see;
But believe it or not,
you won't find it so hot
If you ain't got the do re mi.

Guthrie became famous. He is best remembered for his song "This Land Is Your Land."

▼Woody Guthrie wrote many songs about Okie life.

This famous photo by ▲ Dorothea Lange showed how migrants suffered.

"Hungry and desperate"

Many **Okies** did well in California. Others suffered as they tried to survive. Dorothea Lange was a photographer. She took the photo on page 18. The woman in this photograph is Florence Owens Thompson. She and her seven children lived in a tent. They lived in a muddy pea-pickers camp. Lange remembered how she took the photograph:

> "[I saw] the hungry and desperate mother ... She told me her age—that she was 32. She said that they had been living on frozen vegetables from the ... fields and birds that the children killed. She had just sold the tires from her car to buy food."

Lange wanted to show how farm workers suffered. One of her photos of Thompson appeared in newspapers. It caused Americans to act. Many people showed up at the camp. They brought food and supplies. Thompson had already left. But other **migrant** (traveling) workers got help.

◀ This picture shows photographer Dorothea Lange. Lange photographed the people and places of the Dust Bowl.

The Grapes of Wrath

John Steinbeck worked as a newspaper reporter. He talked to the **migrant** farm workers. This led him to write a book. The book is called *The Grapes of Wrath*. It is the most famous story about **Okie** life.

Steinbeck's awards

In 1940 Steinbeck won the Pulitzer Prize for his book The Grapes of Wrath. *This is the biggest award for a U.S. author. In 1962 he won the Nobel Prize for Literature. This is the highest honor in the world for a writer.*

fictional made-up story

Steinbeck's book is about the Joad family from Oklahoma. The Joads were **fictional** (a made-up story). But thousands of real Okies lived just like the Joads. The Joads' story made many Americans sad. *The Grapes of Wrath* became a huge bestseller. In 1940 it was turned into a popular movie. The billboard in this picture advertised the movie.

▼*Migrant farmworkers lived behind this billboard for* The Grapes of Wrath.

Getting a New Deal

People needed help during the Dust Bowl. The Dust Bowl and **Great Depression** left many people poor. Help came from President Franklin D. Roosevelt. He started the **New Deal**. This was a plan to end the Great Depression.

Roosevelt also wanted to find out why the Dust Bowl had happened. Bad farming was partly to blame. Farmers dug up land. The **drought** made the soil dry. The soil was over-used. It was unprotected against the wind.

The New Deal offered a solution to the problem. The poster on page 23 shows how. Farmers were asked to plant trees in certain places. The trees blocked the wind.

The Civilian Conservation Corps (CCC) was another program. It was also part of the New Deal. The CCC gave young men without jobs a place to work. They planted 200 million trees. CCC workers helped stop soil from being **eroded** (worn down) by the wind.

erode	wear down
New Deal	President Franklin D. Roosevelt s plan to end the Great Depression

Migrant Camps

The **New Deal** also created the Farm Security Administration (FSA). In 1936 the FSA built camps in California. **Migrant** (traveling) workers lived in those camps.

Camp families lived in tents. They also lived in tin cabins. But an FSA camp was much better than an **Okieville**. Most of the FSA camps had showers and bathrooms. Some even had an auditorium. Dances were held there weekly.

This photo shows children▼ at the FSA Tulare migrant camp. It was in Visalia, California.

▲*This photo shows the library at the Tulare migrant camp.*

Many FSA camps had schools. Kids in regular schools made fun of **Okie** kids. But the FSA camp schools were places where they could belong. Okie kids even helped to build the schools. One student remembered:

"It was the first time the children had anything of their own, where all the attention was on them, where they were given the best and they knew everything was for them."

An end and a beginning

In 1941 rain finally came back to the Dust Bowl area. New Deal programs had helped stop the soil from **eroding** (wearing away). These programs also helped educate people. They taught people to plant trees and plants that held soil down. The dust storms ended. Farmers could finally plant **crops** (plants).

The outbreak of ▼ World War II made jobs easier to find.

That same year, the United States entered World War II (1939–1945). The war was another **disaster**. This terrible event cost millions of lives.

But during the war it was easier to find work. The army had to build planes and tanks. The navy had to build ships. People were needed to fight in the war. All of this created new jobs. Those jobs ended the **Great Depression**.

The Dust Bowl and Depression hurt people. Those who survived never forgot. The United States has had hard times since. But nothing has compared to the hard times of the Dirty Thirties.

▼Most young men had to serve in the military during the war.

Quilts of the Dust Bowl

During the Dust Bowl, handmade **quilts** helped poor families in many ways. A quilt is a warm blanket made of two layers of cloth.

First, the quilts let families reuse old, worn-out rags. Women wove them into heavy cloth.

Second, they kept people warm at night. Poor families could not afford to buy blankets.

Third, women could hold quilting parties. They talked and sewed. They also taught one another ways to make fancy patterns.

▼Quilting parties let people talk and spend time with friends.

Lastly, quilts were pretty. Poor families had few ways to decorate their homes. A colorful quilt added life to rooms.

Quilting almost died out after World War II. Blankets became cheap and easy to buy. Few people wanted to make their own. But quilting became popular again in the 1970s. Today, many Dust Bowl quilts are seen as works of art. They even hang in museums!

29

quilt   warm blanket made of two layers of cloth

Glossary

black blizzard huge dust storm

crop plant grown for human use

disaster terrible event

drought lack of rain

erode wear down

fictional made-up story

Great Depression period when many Americans could not find jobs. It lasted from 1929 to 1941.

jalopy old, beat-up car

migrant someone who moves a lot from place to place

New Deal President Franklin D. Roosevelt's plan to end the Great Depression

Okie person fleeing the Dust Bowl

Okieville small camp where Okies lived. They were made up of tents and shacks.

quilt warm blanket made of two layers of cloth

shack poorly built cabin

Want to Know More?

Books to read

- Hesse, Karen. *Out of the Dust.* New York: Scholastic, 1997.

- Isaacs, Sally Senzell. *Life in the Dust Bowl.* Chicago: Heinemann Library, 2002.

- Stanley, Jerry. *Children of the Dust Bowl: The True Story of the School at Weedpatch Camp.* New York: Crown, 1992.

Websites

- http://www.pbs.org/wgbh/amex/dustbowl/index.html
  Visit this PBS website to explore the people and places of the Dust Bowl.

- http://memory.loc.gov/ammem/ndlpedu/features/timeline/depwwii/dustbowl/dustbowl.html
  Visit this Library of Congress website to learn more about the Dust Bowl, the Great Depression, and World War II.

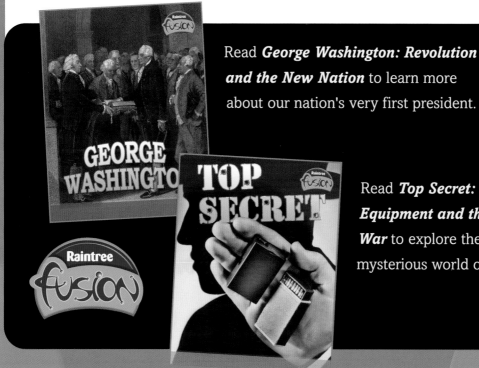

Read *George Washington: Revolution and the New Nation* to learn more about our nation's very first president.

Read *Top Secret: Spy Equipment and the Cold War* to explore the mysterious world of spies.

Index